T0288306

'*mark the dawn* is simply stunni. _
through to the next, and next astounding poem. I love the
intelligence of Jazz Money.' – **Alexis Wright**

'*mark the dawn* is Blak, queer, campfire poetry, pages ablaze.
From its daybreak opening poems until the last page, Jazz
Money's second collection is multiverse, tender and exquisite.'
– **Anne-Marie Te Whiu**

'These poems reveal life in every line, bound by indomitable
truth: language and being are indivisible from Country, and
all its wonder, complexity, beauty, constant ephemerality.
mark the dawn is a (living) book of gentle, visceral masterpieces.'
– **Sara M Saleh**

'Jazz Money's second book is not so much a collection of
poetry as a conjuration, a sentient document of Freshwater
metaphysics. Do not mistake this language for English,
nor this as a work of Australian literature: it is Wiradjuri
literature, the source-code of Country pulsing through
every riparian beat and curve. It is a Wiradjuri blade that
cuts these swift grooves into the coloniser's tongue, a
Wiradjuri weaver who dextrously fashions this vessel for
your weariness, Wiradjuri eros that kindles this cleansing
smoke, Wiradjuri love that animates every syllable and
sings your queer Blak bones into their sovereign vibration.
Read this work aloud in one long exhalation: may this
current carry you where you need to go.' – **SJ Norman**

praise for *how to make a basket*

'Within the pages of this crackling debut collection, Jazz Money guides us through the steps on how to make a basket, a learning seeped in a deep respect for Country; her heart and veins, her soil and spirit. Poetry sings and calls to us on every page, within each line, sometimes quietly, but also with roaring energy. I adore this book, and will cherish having learned from Jazz Money that it takes true love to make a great poem.' – **Tony Birch**

'*how to make a basket* is a lesson written on the body, navigating contours and flows on Country, awakenings and flesh; a delicate constellation of strands reflecting rivers and stars, spilling moonglow and song on the pulse of time. This is a fierce and intimate offering storied through blood and secrets and salt and ash; an exquisite weave of pleasure and pain to carry heartbeats and truths, gifted to ancestors and her every horizon.' – **Natalie Harkin**

'*how to make a basket* harmonises bursts of lyrical raw energy with a melodic call to arms. Striking a dynamic balance between old-worldly adeptness and present-day resonance, Money's is an honest craft and a very promising voice.' – ***The Big Issue***

'It is beautiful and lyrical – I couldn't put this down. Money has a strong sense of form as she finds connection with her ancestors and her Country, feeling the trees, smoke, water, sky and heat all around her.' – ***Readings Monthly***

'Money's poetry is at once tender and sharp, clear-eyed and lyrical. I know I'll return to it again and again.'
– *Sydney Morning Herald*

'A powerful and accomplished debut.'
– **Maxine Beneba Clarke**

'This is a brilliant debut that leaps, lights and lives in tune with the depths of love. Satirical, sensitive and subversive, Jazz Money is a poet to watch.' – **Omar Sakr**

'Jazz Money rebirths the art of storytelling in *how to make a basket*: a fervent compass of language and time, echoing the lines of unceded memories.' – **Yvette Holt**

'Jazz's poetry reminds me love still exists even if my heart is fragmented. She traverses the political landmines (living Blak) and reclaims language so that we know the taste of revival when it is spoken. *how to make a basket* is a series of love letters, a declaration, you are – we are, still here.'
– *Ascension Magazine*

'A luminous and beautifully sculpted, seamless collection of poems that reflects on place and passion. *how to make a basket* builds on the growing canon of work by contemporary Indigenous women poets, yet offers a new, fresh perspective on remembering and forgetting.'
– **2020 David Unaipon Award Judges**

Jazz Money is a Wiradjuri poet and artist producing works that encompass installation, digital, performance, film and print. Their extensive writing and art has been presented, performed and published nationally and internationally. Trained as a filmmaker, their first feature film, *WINHANGANHA* (2023), was commissioned by the National Film and Sound Archive. Jazz's debut poetry collection, the bestselling *how to make a basket* (UQP, 2021), won the David Unaipon Award. Their second collection is *mark the dawn*, which was the recipient of the UQP Quentin Bryce Award in 2024.

JAZZ MONEY

mark the dawn

UQP

First published 2024 by University of Queensland Press
PO Box 6042, St Lucia, Queensland 4067 Australia

uqp.com.au
reception@uqp.com.au

University of Queensland Press (UQP) acknowledges the Traditional Owners and
their custodianship of the lands on which UQP operates. We pay our respects to their
Ancestors and their descendants, who continue cultural and spiritual connections to
Country. We recognise their valuable contributions to Australian and global society.

Cover design by Jenna Lee
Typeset in 11.5/14 pt Bembo Std by Post Pre-press Group, Brisbane
Printed in Australia by McPherson's Printing Group

 University of Queensland Press is supported by the
Queensland Government through Arts Queensland

  University of Queensland Press
is assisted by the Australian
Government through Creative
Australia, its principal arts
investment and advisory body.

A catalogue record for this book is available from the National Library of Australia.

ISBN 978 0 7022 6844 1 (pbk)
ISBN 978 0 7022 6962 2 (epdf)

University of Queensland Press uses papers that are natural, renewable and recyclable
products made from wood grown in well-managed forests and other controlled sources.
The logging and manufacturing processes conform to the environmental regulations of
the country of origin.

for Elijah

so too the sunrise

so too the sunrise
with clarity and promise
of who you will rise to be

so too the breaking night
who knows dance and feast
and then resting

so too the moon
who sees all those standing
at the edge of journey

the moth lifting to light
the glistening nectar of now
the current drifting on

so too us hands held
ready to take the first step
into glory glowing dawn

with the burnished gold light

strike the sparks

into the still air

break this breaking day

for our laughter will become the waterfall

together hands held

with the burnished
gold light

our abundance as though it were honey

don't tell me of the matriarchs by comparing them to kings

I want to hear that love song with the gravel from your belly
about the worlds our women shaped from the molten rock

washed in the sweet water that collects between them thighs

did you see the way they raised homes from the wind
the way they carried our abundance
                                        as though it were honey

there are ways that this love makes and unmakes me daily
blessings that are the tender gift
                                        of responsibility

a community carrying ancient all this knowing
that to hold is to be held and so witness
                                        how it is carried

this love burning in the chest
since the first fires made us

dusk and dawn can be like holding water

sit down soft   here bub
I've been wanting to tell you a story
that begins when the stars were still finding their place in the sky
or when you first took that laugh to your lungs
and told em all
you were ready to begin

sometimes all this living
feels as simple as stepping into a stream
letting the current move through you
across you
beyond
into a story that remembers the contours of your softness
carries knowing to be sipped around bend

but then there's those mornings
when it seems the dawn never calls down the dark
to save you from longing night
and every bird across the valley
cries with a reminder of ones you left behind

there is always upstream
and there is always beyond
but it's that place where the light teaches us transforming
that every bird celebrates in song

dusk and dawn can be like holding water in your cupped hand
enough to drink quick but not to carry home
so bask glowing in the light that moves in swift colour
sent by faraway sky before twilight tips through to the next note

and darkness comes with other teachings
there is brightness bursting
all this exaltation
to show you
that it's the places between binary
the dusk the dawn the you
for which Country saves its most precious glow

another name for mountain

remember when we choked down the salt
that ran from our mothers' backs
felt sure of tomorrow's tomorrow's heartache

this is still the time when rocks carve to the pace of seismic yearning
thrust skyward to mark the night with their love
where rain returns the promise to kiss back all that rupture

everything turns gentle in mist
that's why our aunties weep beautiful
to heal the wounds to soothe the scars

this is how we dance in time to both stone and river
every step knowing the weight of together
so that family becomes another name for mountain

these are not spill marks but tide rushing in

there are fish and long stories
living swimming below the rocks and claypan
places the ancestors placed precious
in the time when the fluid world became firm
the hum of time unspooling across the land
as static in the air

with colour spread out across the sky soft moving
telling us hard moving stories
so keep ya head up and pay attention

time is up shore to shore up truth
trace the line of Country
where of it all comes
dripping splashing leaking
returning

these are not spill marks
but tide rushing in with story to be learnt
across briny mud-rippled flat

this is not wind-worn stone
but the calluses of time tender to shape around all that
grows and knows and exhales its care

it's all shared breath here where the time returns
if you listen right
you can hear the ancestors walking amongst us

there isn't a time before it begins

of course
whitefellas try to acknowledge things
but they do it wrong
they say
   before we begin I'd like to pay my respects
not understanding
that there isn't a time before it begins
   it has all already begun

a spiral in the everywhen as we dance
through all time deep
only as far from our story as Country is from our feet

small soft-bodied things

the world is large and loud
              and we   we are small
soft-bodied things that lean to the sun
                    as flowers do

guided by the most simple demand –
      to be here
            to continue
      to love

to take part in the exquisite mystery
with our faces turned to one another
                  repeating –
      I do not know   I do not know
yet held together
              in that enormous promise

strike the sparks

strike the sparks

★
we
have
a name
for all this
absence
but I won't
speak it here
in these hallowed halls
where so many others
have been taken where
so many others
have been
lost
★ ★
★

       ★
       these
        collectors
       been
        building
       me up
      all crystal
     and palace
    all garden and grand
   making big halls
   big cabinet and ball
    making a place where
      songs go quietness with
   unkeeping where ceremony
goes unordered this-ing
and that-ing muddled by
hands not welcomed
to a knowledge so
  whole true
   loving
    ★ ★ ★
     ★ ★
      ★

★
★ ★★
★ ★ ★
what's this
story palace
you trying to tell
stacked up too big
on a ground trespass
pushing together all pile
and peril hearing the
ancestors creaking
against all wrong
while you been
blocking those
ears all
gone
★ ★
what
knowledge
could be
attempted
in these grand
wantings of
exhibition
that wasn't first
made true in the
plains ebbs and salt
of this land which
grew and spoke
which yielded
as one
★ ★★
★

15

★
★ ★

the night
sky is visible
in the spaces
missing
the star glow
showing all the whole
where we know in
darkness as in light
I begin to sing a little bit
just a whisper really
back to the sharp mark
of those left behind
in trueness
★　★　★
★ ★★
★　　　　　　　　　　★

I know
you told them
I remember how
the lightning struck
the wind howled
sea turned
all violent sicking
I remember the soil
boiling breaching
as all got built up
wrongways
unwelcome
here
★ ★
★

★
★ ★
all this
Country
singing out
to be known
and to know back
those of proper care
hands shaping
timber cut strong
tended with fire
guarded in ochre
the strings formed
with every part known
for there is no debris
no useless mark
and everything
a kin of
shields
canoe and spear
baskets with the
proper names yes
but you collectors
are all full of
forgetting
★   ★ ★
★

★
　★

this
is a site
of blood
and knowing
of bone and
theft
this is
the place
where the hills
been watching
a long time
held warm with the
rhythm of beating feet
where fires
mark the dawn
★　★★　★
★　★　★
★

★
I am fire
and you are
failing us
　★
　★　★

which spirits
strike the sparks
that tear through
the knowledge
of violation?
those living in
cabinet captured or all
them held within
upon beneath
the foundations
of this great hall
who never
granted welcome
to that foreign
step here
★ ★　★
　★ ★

★
you
say gone
we say
forever
as we rise
from the
smoking
earth
★ ★ ★
★ ★
★

since always

and when they question whether
our gorgeous queer bodies
have thrived here since always
probing for 'proof' for 'evidence'
in their written records of dispossession
beat your chest sib
and say 'here'

in the ledger of this history

       everything is accounted for
in the smoke that floats from burning loot
carried on sky-held currents
back to yearning shore

       everything is accounted for
when each mark is made with tender knowing
lines in bloodline tracing
truth against the missing

       everything is accounted for
in the libraries and collections where our makings
go wilfully absent and were never
owed to the glass of their containing

       everything is accounted for
that is why I follow the scent of smoke
not because it will bring back the burnt or dispersed
but because what burns will cleanse
and this continent keeps finding ways to burn and mourn
those who were taken without pathway home

let everything be accounted for

where sun-soaked hands carve song from hard stone
woven tight with hair whose twining memory moves still in the living
held together as nets woven strong to currents yield
stone or ember against wood to carry hollowed everything to hold
rubbed soft with oil until glowing from within
tended with ochre in pattern-known story
strung with shells like a night sky close and closed

let everything be accounted for

that was made of Country who never forgets
in our skins and in our knowings
in your empty palace razed

let everything be accounted for

walkabout (1971)

where the violence of teenage softness swims gentle under the
lingering lens of camera and crew
and the gentleness of dinner becomes violence in contrast

the music swells to tell you that this is all beauty and wrongness
and why it could be her body that the spear is aimed at
a glutton of killing and she might be next

it's the nakedness of the body white and gliding in that dark
against dark against skin so dark to recall the softness that is
missing

where once the body swam brown and smooth
while the skin pink and blistered under high sun marched
through the death-spilt land

and darkness of blood pooled in gully
where whiteness now swims
turned that eden all wrong

the fire inside

1.

all this living is a constant cycle of fire

of ash to shoots to saplings
to life to tinder to smoke to flame
with the beginning begun long ago
and so it goes again

imagine what seeds have been laid here
through all this scorching
imagine what will rise from the ash

2.

ours is a legacy of sifting
through record and return

determining meaning from the demeaning

the eyes that gazed
and in gazing claimed
and in claiming stored
and in all that storied gaze
can we begin to make meaning from the myths they made

myth meant to make this sacred world
all the more easy to claim

3.

the archive holds the archive without body or song
leaves behind trace only
of ceremony and scar

rattling around the documents of our dispossession
is spectre beyond margin and line
the truth of the body that testifies

our body is record of ceremony and scar
written in muscle and flesh and absence
a body beyond the lie of lacking
made of laughter and love and return

4.

returning dignity to document
where hides the fire inside
that could be returned to reignite

did they not know how long fire can burn in the root
how gentle smoke can rise from smoulder
before suddenly all is
alight

and what story would be told
once the power was back in these burning hands
hands that know the shape of these stories
know how to read the secrets coded in the ash

5.

it comes returning all things
story reclaimed in the hidden folds of all that neglect

the body is the body that knows
whose knowing moved
and in moving danced
and in dancing soared
a soaring that sought the story true

we are not the dusty record of absence
we are the soil the air the water the flesh the fire
the whole story is written in the scars
of the body
that continues to dance

the balance of shadow

spread fingers wide

        hold your hand to the light

dip those fingertips

        below the horizon

become the place

        where flesh gives to soil

dissolve the balance

        of shadow

    feel your place within this wholeness
    watch light and see between
    feel light edge into edges
    become that golden warmth expanding

streaking glow
      and colour
           bend upon the break
                expand infinitely
within this deep known place

move beyond the wrongness placed upon this soil
the strangeness of a surface seen
for Country is within
          is around
          is all this

scratch the paint
tear the carpet
destroy all that was built unwelcome
        and reveal the marks of here

from above I see
        I see us in river light flung splashing
                a wider birth
every loop to join another
                and the weave goes
        deep and deeper

as you dance
                        the lines will blur
as you sing
                        the land will stir
as you move
                        within all this
you continue returning
an ever-strong net of us and here and home

        us
        here
        home

into the still air

if that ghost is still here come morning

*

if that
ghost is
still here
come morning
brew a hot cup
go out walking
with the memory
of those you
couldn't
heal

*

every night
comes with
new intention
but I don't know
how to read the wind
and this saltwater
has me thirsty for
a current that
knows my
return

*

★

sister
I've been
trying to listen
to this story but
every word
comes out
backwards
and every shadow
meets in long dark
where we go
disappearing

★

step
careful
there's rules
for whistling night
and stronger ones
that can't be taught
if you didn't
grow small
under the eyes
of moonlit knowings
there's places
I didn't
go in
time

★

*

this city
thudded
over site sacred
curls with ghost
watch how
certain places
bubble with
horror or
yearning

*

I'm looking
at these maps
gazing from below
I'm walking with
my ghosts
upon grid
over sewer
and drain
sister
we're marvelling
at shadows writ
upon those dreams
by those
who walk
here
still
*

outback icarus

watch the boy fall sky to dust and through
he doesn't land on that promised confetti
but instead feels the crunch
something that slips between dreams
and cannot be held in morning light
landing hard on a cold hard thing

sounds like a truck tearing along the highway
seen by the Country it crosses unseeing
small bird smashed in the shimmering grille
desperate for a way to get out of this town
like a cricket bat turned tired
yelling out in boxing day backyards of almost and could have
        years gone almost and he could have been a star –

     cuz, is it true
that you can move away and slip into a new skin
polish up the nasal of your accent
and find ways to never tell the full story
of the violence you will learn the name for in the city
     what is it that they say
it's only once there's a distance between yourself and poverty
that you might see it was there all along

maybe hunger lives in the back shed
maybe it lives under those creaking floors
and if you wait long enough in that city
you might even begin to recall housing insecurity and a black eye
as some sort of ridgy-didge bullshit badge of genuine
        ascendence

       I heard em whisper
did you see him before the fall
two fists raised and back gleaming
a proper champion
for us eyes to gaze upon
maybe that uncle built him up wrongways inside this labyrinth
       but here's the thing
I am so sick of you force-feeding
those myths of elsewhere upon this soil
where we have story plenty
and it doesn't end like this

you wrote him in to fall
but I can see him rising

it sounds like a whistle in dawn light
the call of soft returning
it's dark out with only the headlights
to reveal feather and confetti falling
       but yes, cuz, still the night parrot sings

it looks like a man returning
adjusting the flaking ghost gum print
hanging proud above the laundry sink

and if you look at him just right in the city light glow of elsewhere
I can see that story true

they said falling
but I say rising
I say floating
say returning

all a homeland

the performance is survival
the performance is for an audience who knows no better
the people remain sacred
the rain cloud bursts

maybe we're all a homeland of survival and divinity
maybe we've been walking a map laid in the sand a million times over
migratory birds know air currents they've never flown within
will follow a bone memory and return to impossible origins

carve out the space
where quietness waits
this is the monument in absence
the performance is the monument

this city built upon sandstone violence
yield yourself into land
and hear the echo deep of where your heart is buried

can all this Country
taken without ceremony
removed without song
be returned
can this city dissolve
and each stone
with knowing
find its way back to where it belongs
and the final birdsong in light retreating
guide us home

some generosities

where does the wind begin
and how to make   my body   fit
into the spaces left   in the hollowed trees

I want to surrender to the   clay and ash   of this landscape
let the paper daisies remember
only a song

there has been a story carrying   every night   from the inland
see here   the branches contour against the path it cleaves

when overcome   I push my toes   into the grit of this place
notice each flower gathered   petalled and leafed

the generosity to keep this wholeness together
when every shifting wind   is an invitation
to fall   apart

there was rain in the ways of wind crying

there was rain in the ways of wind crying

the sound of long deep wanting came before the drops
the smell of far and thirst came before the sound

and before the smell before the sound
before the drops
was waiting
the rain had not been called

.   "   ;   , '   ,

in all times
land and sky water and people
all known and all not seen
kept harmony held just so

in the always of now and then
has been dance song ceremony care
knowings held
where people and water meet

and so
rain comes when it hears calling
and so
when the singing went quiet
the rain waited

'   ,   ; ; '   ;

all gentle all rage all water cycling
clouds listen in the way of what the land says back
in the cool of night
in the rivers and trees exhaling

but slowly whispers of fires carry on the breeze
a burnt needing that tells of healing not had
dust and sand that sting
where water soothing is missing

those who had settled the land
the people who came without the proper ways
turned sweet small flower to grass all wrong
hoof to trample
a song not sung
and disrespect to all this sacred

                    ' , ;; '
                 ;, ' , "

where are the birds who call in water joy
the frogs who know of rain and emerge in blinking wetness
the sands and seeds who form and bloom in rhythm
where is the water to water our soul

and when those clouds came appearing
after so long without care and summon
the rain saw all the harshness of neglect
heard the tell of too much too little and no song

when rain came returning
it was in fury devastation
in the crying winds carving each place beloved
water rapid moving pain
where flooding falls and the earth gives away for cleansing

in flood we follow to find
all the ways the rain needs us
and all the ways we mourn

saw a ghost

saw a ghost
become a ghost
create a ghost

begin

break this breaking day

mardi gras rainbow dreaming

ʃ⊃ ✿•_•✿⌐⊃ (ˠ)

the BWS is now a BWyaassssssS as in yass queen as in yasssss gay pride as in yass we co-opted this lingo from black queer communities on the other side of the world as in BeerWineSpirits is now a place to drink down some black queer liberation on land stolen that locks up blak queer bodies if maybe they've had a bit too much BeerWineSpirits but won't lock up the others who snarl as you walk down the street hand in hand with ya misso on ya way to have a drink

(⊃ℚ◡◔)⊃ ♥ ≧◔◡◕≦

GayTM it's like an ATM but it's gayer holds your hand after but doesn't leave a number or maybe moves in on tuesday or maybe pays for medication yours or nan's or someone else's or helps get some kid a mental health care plan to figure out why their body don't seem right but won't grant rights and won't write a cheque and won't write to government about bodies that don't fit between two tick-boxes but will give you the option for a receipt thank you see you next time don't forget your card don't forget your cash don't forget your yasssss queen

≧★‿★≦ (∕●ꈊ●)∕*:·˚ ✧

and the google map shows the route in rainbow to the stadium
where exec gays and clever rich straights can have front
row seats behind the gate to the genuine gays and all those
genuine straights who thought it would be so cute to be on
the corporate float this year and march alongside the police
who would absolutely never systematically target the queer
community and who are absolutely not built on a legacy of
doing just that and who absolutely don't uphold a colony that
enforces an ideology that makes no space for non-normative
bodies just ask the next lot oh yay it's the liberal party what
a special day what a lovely float thanks for spending all that
money so everyone could have a vote

(ɔ˘ ³(^‿^c)]:-> :^)

instagram is for mardi gras and google is for mardi gras and
absolut is for mardi gras and vodafone is for mardi gras and
sydney is for mardi gras a tourism campaign and mardi gras is
for profits under a rainbow banner that holds no one up but
gives enough rope to make sure that there is one version of a
rainbow and it fits the gaze of execs who had to work hard to
be so correct and even went to their cousin's wedding yes two
grooms and look this is what the community want and look
this is a community with cash and look money is for mardi gras
and mardi gras was a protest but protest isn't sexy when it's hard
or anti-excess so you can wrap up your bigotry in glitter and
call it progress for a weekend and none of these corporations
speak up when they come for our rights but hashtag loveislove
when everything is over won and done

(/●ㄱ●)/ (^o^) (✿ꈍ‿ꈍ)

the blaks get down on a knee and it doesn't make the broadcast
and the cops get run out run onto and it doesn't make the
broadcast and the community floats get their thirty seconds and
the corporate floats get their seventy seconds and the protest
before the march is the family event that gets run out run onto
by those cops who tried to block queer-loving protest and on
the walk home down oxford street dreaming we get heckled
and listen to others screaming and men with iphones ask us
to kiss for their private archive and strangers with long-range
lenses take photos for who knows what archive not asking yass
queen mardi gras dreaming sydney wears its corruptness never
fearing and no need to shame your rum colony feeding rum
colony breeding more cops who can run out run onto those
who can't afford to pay thank you thank you sydney for our
special diluted day

(ꃰ.ꃰ) (_!_) (^‿^)

51

queers in hell is a return to the classics

queers in hell is a return to the classics
we all know hell is for queers
not because queerness sends you to hell
but because queerness is desire and heat
and a celebration of all bodies beyond binary beyond neatness
beyond control

hell is for queers because we all look fabulous in red
and appreciate camp interiors
that's why we look so good at the club
painted black mirror panel reflecting an infinity of sin delicious
of straps of leather of bodies dimpled with desire

hell is for queers because no one understands style
like the devil and a butch dyke
the gnashing teeth of pleasure
the embrace of transgression
the serpent's kiss
the song of the underworld at the tips of our needing fingers

Lil Nas X slid down that silver pole moonbeam of sin into the
waiting lap of satan
to free us from the threat of being dragged
and as all those who perform know
it's not punishment if you find yourself in the hell of your choosing
with head high heels high tits high

the reclamation of hell is the safe space of desire
so yes daddy yes when you call me by your name
I absolve the shame and threat of your devil
and return to the classics of desire
hell is for queers of course
because we are the ones to start the fire

out at night eatin' cars

the summer the world turned eighteen
we drove around with a blondie cd stuck in the player
for months we learnt the rise and fall of debbie's range
that's why each sticky-thighed passenger
still knows every word to rapture
on thursdays we would shoplift in our spares
until the incident with the blue beaded purse
made our habits go underground
I tasted a cheeseburger learnt suburban rituals
wrappers strewn on the backseat with other forms of longing
tasting like the fantasy of adulthood for a dirt road kid

the summer we turned eighteen
I yearned to be yearned for
to make sense of my desire
to have a place in the constellation of someone else's trash
in those days I assumed I would die in a car
and with jittery acceleration I worried I would die a virgin
I cared deeply about that status
until it changed and there is no word for the time after
my fear shifting then to dying without ever being in love

nothing pierces a teenager like a guitar solo
between the coke bottles and chocolate wrappers
gathering under the feet of our liberation
I would go and hold her hand now
say that love will come crashing in without invitation
this road stretches all the way until it comes back again

and so perhaps that's why we drive the long way home
mouthing along to the lyrics one more time
to catch the spectre of sunset
to become the mote caught in the vanishing rays
to inhabit for a moment the possibilities that still surround us

lucky country

darling
a dollar in the pocket is worth ten
in patriotic investment on these girt and golden shores
in fair australia where we sing australia fair
for all those who have a fair go get a dollar
unless you're not so fair
or sing that praise song backwards
refusing that dollar soaked in the blood gold and horror
of all that this land never gave willingly

darling
they sent the devil in first when they tried to steal this land
and in his hand
a golden dollar
a golden fleece
a golden promise
of golden shores and all that which can be fairly stolen

darling
in fairness
maybe it's time we learnt that dollar undone
is the song of freedom on these lips
and that fairness comes to land where gold comes returning
placed back into soil that grew all this fortune fair

post glitch

we're   post   glitch
and   you   already   know   this   is   deliberate
a   breeze   moves   through   the   server
that   began   when   the   digital   frontier   went   live
and   living   lowered   binary   against   ancestral
placed   basket   on   data   upstream
we're   post   glitch
hear   the   true   languages   coded   on   the   tongues
of   the   digital   native   born

the sound that marks the change

there is a moment before history
as four men assemble with their cardboard and corduroy
waiting for the eyes of the world to focus
on a patch of grass opposite the law

there is a sound when a beach umbrella
is pushed into cropped lawn
when the beauty of clear eyes lift
and a fist is raised on crisp morning

there is a sound when boot meets skull
when a wrist is cuffed in cold steel
belts heavy with baton lug and lurch in unison
and yet rising voices chant on

but this is not a story I can tell
I was not there

I did not hear the umbrella open
I did not chant with my arms locked
as men in starched uniforms
pressed down beat down tore down

I sit in the aftermath of legacy
I live in the world after the beach umbrella
in a time when a fire still burns
and hot cup of tea is waiting on that same lawn

there is a rhythm to resistance
there is a sound to legacy

and there is a moment before
when four young men
decide to change the world
and then there is everything that comes after

for our laughter will
become the waterfall

mama's onions

my mother taught me how to make whole the world with food
baby she said cooking is how you tell people you love them
so you should do it slowly and you should do it well
and you should do it every day

there was a time when I was sad and filled my life
with the pungent smells of home
because I was far away from the backyard lemons I knew
and I missed my mother

every time I chop an onion I am reminded of her
baby you don't need to dice it finely
if you cook it for long enough
baby always toast your seeds to release the flavour
and olive oil with butter will stop the butter burning

food is a language we all speak
so baby you better make sure food for the people you love
is singing

gentle human gestures

all the ways I love you
and all the ways I am
waiting in the valley by
the river hoping for
gentle human
gestures

every day it grows this love

our laughter has ancestors rattling the stars to join us
our singing is ringing from the inland out to sea
the dancing has even the dust leaping in applause

and every day it grows, this love
            every day it grows

I want my babies to hold precious
            every moment we marched for them

for every sacrifice our Elders made
            to be cherished and carved into our histories

for when my babies are here
I do not want them to know the same horrors
            of then and now

that these struggles will be memories
that we must not forget
            as the time begins to stretch from our triumphs

a new dawn is coming and we
            keep laughing in our joy
            singing in our truth
            dancing in our futures

we keep holding each other close
we keep marching towards tomorrow

where every one of us is known
and all time is precious

and every day it grows, this love
every day it grows

sky born

there is a river
flowing above our heads
rising from all the
world's tree-born breath
ancestral pathways to travel
these airborne tides
follow the seed
borne away on
trade winds
we cannot grow
alone
~
in that river
flowing amongst our cloudscape
water moving backwards
through our skies
on currents flow
our water our hopes
in the air beneath our feet
we're breathing clear to water
we're finding our kin
sending new spirits
planting the seeds

campfire

mind that lady stepping down from the stars
beneath this yoke of leaves

                        let's see what can be told

er la   listen to this one
sit down here bub stretch out long and lovely
let those eyes go heavy soft and close

set that hand outstretching towards stars that reflect in eyes and mouth
watch the moon rise from your upturned palm

there is a wide yellowing river dissolving into horizon
there is a night sky strung out with tiny shells
hold one to your ear
can you hear the whispers of a dark quiet

                            of a long ago

it will begin with song in the throat
spiralling down carried upon smoke
shifting constellation star glow

feel with your mouth a joy as you learn true words
whisper to the moths that tell of coming seasons
join them in feast upon that great comb of honey
towards the birds that tell of tomorrow's light
drop down between the shadows of the moon
a river carved ancestral will show you the way

you're slipping through the dark places of campfire
sinking into those singing stars and all the dark spaces in-between
following that lady made of night through cloud until dawn
until you come returning

glowing
rested
strong

all this wonder

it took some time to see you
weren't gone

instead you had reimagined yourself
back into the breath of this breeze

the whirling birds and all the ways
we love them

your heart now beating in the trees
who know quiet without longing

I know you when I step in freshwater
when I gaze up at the stars where we have always lived

it took some time to see you
here with me

in all this wonder
and the ways of love

together hands held

the outline

I lifted you into the night air
a wing where once the stars had shone
in absence I saw the outline of sacred
in absence of light
the world was whole

soft falling world

of course all things carry life and death held together

that's why I lift you up   as a vessel filled to brim with spring water
                      to the parched tired pilgrims of my lips
      and drink you greedy
          all at once and then

we're falling to earth so very slowly my love

      and there is only forever   and our ancestors
         on the other side of this divide

all I know to do is hold you as tightly
                     as lichen clings to the eternal stone
      turning all things solid into
         softness into soil   into habitat and home

this is the way our love holds great floodwaters strong
         by saying
           we need one another   all all all
      if we're to make any sense in this soft falling world

carried towards glowing tomorrow

that   current   pulling   out

with   whispering   promise

of   new   dawn   new   horizon   old   song

small   blossom   drifts   soft   stream   ways

where   sunlight   waits   in   quiet   bloom

it   all   keeps   flowing   keeps   growing

moving   through   and   on

story   gathered   and   gather   story

in   infinite   becoming   and   ceaseless   river

carried   away   in   old   learnings

towards   glowing   tomorrow

on   water   and   song

bodies made of night

when
you feel
yourself
dissolving
into nothing
more than the
passing breeze
surrender to that
moonlit promise
ascend to the place
where rivers rise to
meet your
waiting
breath
flowing in through
your mouth pouring
to fill your very self
with softness
with moon glow
with memory
darling
we're just bodies
made of night
reflected in water
we're just rivers
flowing towards
each other's
floodplain
desperately
seeking
the sea

listen up, bub

well this was back when we used to talk about gender as a binary, and you would have to tick these little boxes that said male or female, as though that was a fixed thing and as though that somehow affected your ability to like, sign in to a website, or to get a concession card for public transport … So you actually needed to pay for public transport, or, now that I think about it, you needed to pay for everything. If you wanted to go somewhere, or turn on the light or even turn on the tap. It's bizarre to think about it now, but this was back when the government had privatised all the public assets and sold them off to private corporations, and then they were making the public pay for infrastructure that they already owned … Oh well, the government, that was a bit of a misguided one, bub. Good intentions, I think, at first. It was meant to be this system of democracy, but it didn't really work. Governments could be very cruel and vindictive, didn't represent values or even advocate for decency. And the whole thing was owned by newspapers and geared towards keeping rich people rich … Newspapers? Oh, well, newspapers. They were kinda like the internet, but before the Digital Revolution & Cyber Sovereignty Act. But, uh, have you ever heard of the idea of a celebrity? Or an influencer? Or, um, fake news? Nah, nah don't bother looking it up, it's nothing important. But before fake news and celebrities were made redundant in the Digital Anarchy Movement we had these things called newspapers … This was all back before the wealth was redistributed and people were still allowed to own land, and own, you know, people's time. Can you imagine it? Land ownership! Exactly, bub, if you owned the land you owned the body. Well, was that a good system for keeping the colonisers in power! But you've learnt about all this and the Blak Republic Revolution at the community knowledge centre, yeh? ... Yeh, exactly, it all came just after we finally stopped burning fossil fuel for power, and before we shut down all those factories that were still pumping carbon into the atmosphere ... Don't look at me like that – it's over now! And to be honest, we got there just in the nick of time. And yeh, these new technologies that are made of cornstarch don't last more than a year, but the weird thing was, neither did the smart phones full of rare earth metals and at least you can bury these ones in the garden once you're done ... So, rare earth metals? Bub, have you heard of mining? Where like white folk would come along and point at something and say 'that's mine', and then they'd literally rip out of the earth all the things that had been placed there by the ancestors. Metals and minerals, all that sort of thing ... You've heard of oil, right? Not like olive and coconut, but the stuff made out of, uh, dinosaurs? Yeh, true! Dinosaurs! Look, to be honest I never really understood how most of it worked anyway but all this was before the age of 3D printing. Yeh, used to be you couldn't print anything at home! Just paper, really ... Well, actually now you mention it, did you know that meat used to come from killing animals? Nah, I'm serious! And we cleared all this bushland so that animals could just like, be out in these big, hot, open paddocks getting fat before we killed them. Just keeping animals to kill them – that was the whole system. Well, yeh, most of that bush between here and your grandparents' place was grazing for animals. Yeh, exactly, all that beautiful bush where your uncle goes to get tucker with you. You know the big lake near your grandparents' place? Yeh, that one that's full of all those birds. Well, when I was your age that spot used to just be a dust bowl, all brown and ripped up out of the ground. Not many birds in that place. Thing called a quarry. Well, it had this polluted little bit of water at the bottom and, true god, if you'd gone into it you would have gotten sick. But this was before the rivers were rehabilitated and recognised as sacred by everyone ... It was a very different way of thinking about water back then, and of thinking about the land. Well, not for the Blakfullas, but you know, it was before everyone else learnt how to listen to Blakfullas ... First Nations Sovereignty wasn't like it is now. Remember how I told you about how the white settlers used to decide what literally everyone got to do? They hadn't even been here that long ... Bub, you wouldn't believe it. They used to put people in prison for things like being poor or being sick! Prison? Oh well, that, that was terrible! Not like a metaphor, like a little box they'd just lock folk up in ... You know how your Deedee has that t-shirt that says 'abolition' on it? No, no, it's not a band. Or it might be a band, but I don't think that's what the t-shirt is about. The t-shirt is about getting rid of this prison industrial complex ... So, we used to think that people committed crimes as individuals instead of, like, looking at the systemic problems that were creating these issues. I don't quite know how to explain it but instead of, like, fixing the problems we'd just lock up the individual, even though the crime was nearly always a societal issue, something that the poor bugger couldn't help ... This was during a time when everyone was obsessed with this thing called money and if you didn't have enough your life would be totally different to those who had a lot of it. But the people with lots wouldn't share it and would penalise the folk without it for not having more ... It was terrible, the whole system was built on extracting wealth from sacred bodies and sacred places. And the rich folk were powerful, and powerful folk could tell everyone else what to do, even though there were actually a lot more poor folk than rich folk ... Again, it was this system called government that was supposed to mean one thing but usually was the exact opposite of democracy. I mean, not long before you was born it was actually illegal for two women to be recognised as a couple. Can you imagine that? Having a system with laws, and the laws were concerned with things like who could be in love with who and how. You could have had a heteronormative mum and a dad if the government had had their way. They were obsessed with controlling peoples bodies, the government … Did I tell you about gender? Binary? No, not code. More like the body, and the way we decide to make our own dawn …

notes

'our abundance as though it were honey' first appeared online in 2023 under the title 'ember' in a video recording made for Aje to mark International Women's Day.

'these are not spill marks but tide rushing in' was written in response to Judy Watson's exhibition *mudunama kundana wandaraba jarribirri* at QAGOMA 2024.

'there isn't a time before it begins' is after Amrita Hepi's performance work *Rinse*: 'In the beginning there are worlds and worlds ending. In the beginning there is, and always was, ancestors.'

'strike the sparks' is after Jonathan Jones's 2016 public artwork *barrangal dyara (skin and bones)*. The similarity of the title to Sharon Olds's collection *Strike Sparks: Selected Poems, 1980–2002* is coincidental.

'since always' is indebted to Sandy O'Sullivan's essay, 'No Cession'.

'in the ledger of this history' was written in response to Jonathan Jones's body of research and exhibition called *untitled: transcriptions of country*, which charted, amongst other things, sacred objects taken from the east coast of Australia that were subsequently lost or destroyed in France at the end of the Napoleonic era.

'walkabout (1971)' is a response to the film of the same name.

'the fire inside' originally formed the structural scaffold of the feature film *WINHANGANHA* commissioned by the National Film and Sound Archive of Australia. It was written and subsequently adapted while considering the complexity of First Nations people after consulting colonial documents filled with misinformation that nonetheless reconnect us with our stories.

'the balance of shadow' is after Brook Garru Andrew's installation *DIWIL* at Murray Art Museum Albury in 2021.

'outback icarus' was written for Dean Cross's exhibition *Icarus, my Son* at Goulburn Regional Art Gallery and Carriageworks in 2021. This poem was originally published with the titled 'still the night parrot sings'.

'all a homeland' was written for a video piece of the same name commissioned by the Sydney Opera House for *Shortwave* in 2022.

'mardi gras rainbow dreaming' was written in response to the 2021 Sydney Gay and Lesbian Mardi Gras Parade.

'queers in hell is a return to the classics' is after Lil Nas X and the Art Gallery of NSW's European galleries in 2022.

'out at night eatin' cars' borrows the title from the 1980 song 'Rapture' by Blondie. The text was inspired by Hanif Abdurraqib's poem 'When We Were 13, Jeff's Father Left The Needle Down On A Journey Record Before Leaving The House One Morning And Never Coming Back'.

'post glitch' was originally commissioned and presented on the digital poetry platform *Crawlspace*. It is best experienced at crawlspace.cool/post-glitch.

'the sound that marks the change' was written to celebrate and commemorate fifty years of the Aboriginal Tent Embassy protest on the lawns of Parliament in Canberra, ACT.

'campfire' is an adpated poem from the sleep story 'Bilabang' for the *Dreamy* series by Common Ground.

'carried towards glowing tomorrow' was a commissioned piece for A.N.'s 30th birthday.

'bodies made of night' was written for the band Velvet Trip and appears on their album *Harmony Blooms*.

'listen up, bub' originally appeared within a visual art work of the same name in the *Here: After* exhibition at Fairfield Museum curated by Tian Zhang in 2021.

'it's always been always' is an ongoing series within my art practice. The first iteration – a blue neon text piece – was hung in the *NO FALSE IDOLS* exhibition at 4A Gallery, curated by Con Gerakaris, in 2022.

acknowledgements

Much of this writing and thinking took place on the lands of the Gadigal and Wangal peoples. Mandaang guwu, thank you, to the custodians who have cared always for this place and for the many Countries that spread across this beautiful continent. Mandaang guwu to my Wiradjuri Elders, and to all keeping Country strong.

This book was written in a time of trying to reckon with many tumultuous events and compounding incidents of colonial violence taking place on the global stage. *mark the dawn* began as an attempt to figure how we mark time, how we make sense of our moment and how we reckon with the legacies we inherit. In particular, how First Nations, People of Colour, queer, disabled, diasporic and marginalised people show up with the astounding courage to live with joy and love and wonder, even in a world of violence. And so this book is written with gratitude to everyone who lives in those complex truths.

These poems have been informed by my practice as an artist and filmmaker and, as such, I am indebted to thinkers and practitioners in those spaces. I want to thank Indigenous activists globally who fight for sovereignty every day here in so-called 'Australia' and all around the world. Free Palestine.

The earliest draft of this book took form while studying a Master of Creative Writing at Western Sydney University. Thank you to my supervisor, Kate Fagan, for the guidance and patience in submitting that body of work. Thank you to Sandy O'Sullivan and Jeanine Leane (for both being deadly academics that I admire greatly) who assessed that thesis and provided valuable feedback that helped shape the final version of *mark the dawn*.

To Ellen van Neerven, it is a joy to be edited by you, thank you, my friend. To UQP, thank you for believing in this book, and in particular to Aviva Tuffield who has known it since its early beginnings and to Yasmin Smith for the sharp eyes. Alexis, SJ, Sara and Anne-Marie, thank you for being early readers and endorsers of this book, I admire each of you and am honoured. To Jenna, for another stunning cover.

This book was written with financial support from Creative Australia (formally the Australia Council for the Arts) and with residency support at Bundanon in 2022. Thank you to Natalie Harkin for being my mentor during the term of the Dreaming Award.

Thank you to all the editors and commissioners of the publications where many of these poems first entered the world, sometimes in different forms or with different titles: *Art Monthly Australasia*, *Arts of the Working Class*, *Cordite*, *Crawlspace*, the National Film and Sound Archive of Australia, Oranges and Sardines Foundation, Red Room Poetry, *Tart* and *un Magazine*.

I am lucky to have a writing life that is far from solitary. Thank you to the Varuna writing group led by Ellen van Neerven and attended by Jeanine, Jasmin, Mel, Jenny and Neika. Thank you, Anne-Marie Te Whiu, for helping me find the title of this collection. To the Bankstown Poetry Slam community, thank you for very literally embodying everything that is meaningful and beautiful about poetry and for welcoming me into your world. Thank you too to Knowledge of Wounds (SJ Norman and Joseph Pierce) for modelling the ways that First Nations knowledge exchange systems can take place on an intimate and global scale. I learn so much.

Finally, thank you to my family – I love you all so much. Elijah, this book is dedicated to you, spectacular teacher of what it is to live in truth and beauty. And to Jenn, my darling, our lives together is the greatest gift I could have ever received – thank you for a life bathed in dawn light.

Winner of the UQP Quentin Bryce Award 2024

mark the dawn **by Jazz Money**

About the UQP Quentin Bryce Award

The Honourable Dame Quentin Bryce AD CVO is an alumna of The University of Queensland, where she completed a Bachelor of Arts and a Bachelor of Laws before becoming one of the first women admitted to the Queensland Bar. In 1968 Quentin Bryce became the first woman appointed as a faculty member of The University of Queensland's Law School. From 2003 to 2008 she served as the twenty-fourth Governor of Queensland, and from 2008 to 2014 she was the twenty-fifth Governor General of Australia, the first woman to hold the office.

In addition to her professional roles, Quentin Bryce has always been a strong supporter of the arts and Australia's cultural life and is an ambassador for many related organisations, including the Stella Prize and the Indigenous Literacy Foundation. Across many decades she has championed The University of Queensland Press (UQP), its books and authors.

To honour and celebrate her impressive career and legacy, The University of Queensland and UQP have jointly established the UQP Quentin Bryce Award. The award recognises one book on UQP's list each year that celebrates women's lives and/or promotes gender equality.

The inaugural recipient of the award in 2020 was Ellen van Neerven's poetry collection *Throat*, which went on to be recognised in multiple prizes, including winning Book of the

Year at the 2021 NSW Premier's Literary Awards. In 2021 the award went to Sarah Walker's exceptional collection of essays, *The First Time I Thought I Was Dying*, with its examination of our unruly bodies and minds, and the limitations of consent, intimacy and control. In 2022 the recipient was Mirandi Riwoe's dazzling story collection, *The Burnished Sun*, with its focus on women, especially those who are marginalised and disenfranchised, while in 2023 it was Angela O'Keeffe's *The Sitter*, which reimagines the life of Hortense Cezanne while intricately examining the tension between artist and subject, and between the stories told about us and the stories we choose to tell. *The Sitter* won the 2024 NSW Premier's Literary Award for fiction. The recipient of the 2024 UQP Quentin Bryce Award is Jazz Money's much-anticipated second poetry collection, *mark the dawn*.

'As a long-time reader and lover of poetry I was delighted to be able to select a work of poetry as the UQP Quentin Bryce Award recipient for 2024. Jazz Money's second collection, *mark the dawn*, is a moving, joyful and life-affirming work that shines with love for her Country, her people and the power of community to connect and embrace us. This is a book I will return to again and again, for solace, for inspiration and for a line or two to share with others.'
– Dame Quentin Bryce

how to make a basket by Jazz **Money**

Winner of the David Unaipon Award 2020

Simmering with protest and boundless love, Jazz Money's David Unaipon Award-winning debut poetry collection, *how to make a basket*, examines the tensions of living in the Australian colony today. By turns scathing, funny and lyrical, Money uses her poetry as an extension of protest against the violence of the colonial state, and as a celebration of Blak and queer love. Deeply personal and fiercely political, these poems attempt to remember, reimagine and re-voice history.

Writing in both Wiradjuri and English language, Money explores how places and bodies hold memories, and the ways our ancestors walk with us, speak through us and wait for us.

'Jazz Money is a poet to return to again and again.' – *Readings Monthly*

'A book that lies at the intersection of womanhood, Indigenous history, settler colonialism, queer love and memory. Money's voice is lyrical yet sharp, moving through land, language and love as protest against colonial violence.' – *Books+Publishing*

ISBN 978 0 7022 6338 5